Praise for
The Traveling Saleslady Meets Live Bedbugs

There are hundreds of sales books out there, but this easy-to-read book is a MUST-read for sales managers—especially those starting out in a new sales position or starting their sales career. I would also recommend to any sales professional at any level who is looking for new motivation and perspective!

Deanna brings years of professional and personal experience and delivers them in bite-size nuggets that are simple to understand and engaging. She reminds us of essential traits that are important to a successful sales career such as passion, mindset and lifelong learning that are often missed in traditional sales training or tend to become overlooked in day to day sales activities.

—*Marybeth Fasciano,*
New England Account Manager,
Chemglass Life Sciences

I thoroughly enjoyed reading this book! I just loved how Deanna incorporated her bedbug fiasco with thoughtful sales tips. In thirty-five years of sales, I've been through numerous sales trainings, some helpful and most just not that inspiring. This was the most engaging book I've read on sales with a fun twist!
—*Barb DiSenso, Sales Operations, Fomerra*

As a sales and marketing professional, I've read dozens of books related to the field. This is one of the most original and informative books I've read in regard to sales. Written by a professional road warrior who has truly lived the sales life, it provides real-world examples of effective sales practices. And who would have thought a close encounter with bedbugs would lead to a genuinely engaging read! Though the concepts outlined in the book are easy to understand, they are not often applied by salespeople. Give this a read and watch how you'll stand out from the crowded sales field and find passion for your work. Highly recommend it."

—***Colleen Cowette***, *marketing and sales expert with twenty-five years of experience in B2B and B2C*

The Traveling Saleslady Meets Live Bedbugs

The Traveling Saleslady Meets Live Bedbugs

Sales Tips Galore for Road Warriors

Deanna L. Vigliotta

ISBN: 979-8-9910611-1-7 (softcover)
ISBN: 979-8-9910611-2-4 (ebook)

Cover design: Valentina Pino
Editing and typesetting: Creative Editorial Solutions

TheTravelingSaleslady.com

I dedicate this book to my prior and current sales teammates, whose camaraderie and shared experiences have shaped my path. I also dedicate this book to Joyce Marier, a beacon of positivity in life. Additionally, I extend my gratitude to United Airlines, Jet Blue, and Delta for consistently providing reliable Wi-Fi and electrical outlets in every seat. These amenities have allowed me to write, reflect, and gain invaluable perspective at 37,000 feet in the air.

CONTENTS

FOREWORD

I met Deanna Vigliotta in 2014 when we worked together at a national imaging company. She started working for the company a few months after I started, and we quickly became fast friends. I soon left the organization, but through the years we stayed in touch as we continued to work in the same industry. When Deanna reached out to me about completing a lifelong dream to write a book, I was intrigued. I became very curious about how bedbugs could be related to sales.

There are many different books on the fundamentals of sales. We as sellers are always trying to find the next best kept secret to sales. We want something that is simple and clearly defines the process. Over the years, the process of sales has changed. The process for a buyer has changed, and buyers now have more information at their fingertips. As sales professionals, we must adapt to this knowledge and truly understand the buyer's pain point and what is important to them.

In this book, *The Traveling Saleslady Meets Live Bedbugs*, Deanna provides valuable insight on sales tips and examples of how to help move the sales cycle forward. She gives real life examples of the sales process she went through as the "new buyer" and expectations that she wanted from a salesperson within an organization. She does this in a simplistic and humorous way. While I hope to never have the pleasure or experience of acquiring bedbugs, please trust that all readers and especially sales road warriors will be more informed related to the connection between sales and bedbugs!

—Darnetta Daire,
Senior Manager, Sales Enablement

INTRODUCTION

Outside of the death of my father and attending funerals of other friends and family members, I really can't think of a more awful experience I have been through in my fifty-nine years of life. In hindsight, I guess that makes me fortunate to have had a pretty happy life overall. Yes, I should count my blessings and I do, but I hope that sharing what happened to me in early 2023 may save other professional salespeople, or anyone else who travels frequently, from having to go through the agony I went through as I encountered and tried to get rid of bedbugs.

To begin, I'll share a little bit about myself to give you some background. First and foremost, my husband and I are very clean people. We have been married for twenty-six years. My husband is an elementary school teacher, and I have been in outside sales and sales management for my entire career. My husband and I have lived in the same house in Florida for the last nineteen years. It's a modest, two-thousand-square-foot home with four bedrooms and two bathrooms. We have two wonderful sons, a twenty-six-year-old and a twenty-three-year-old. My husband and I are extremely proud of them, and we still all enjoy each other's company. We also have one cat named Penny. Side note, she is a love!

Throughout the years—especially when our children were young —there definitely were times when our house was messy. It was never truly dirty, but there were numerous times over the years when our interior rooms needed to be dusted, vacuumed, and decluttered. There were many Saturdays when I would exclaim to my husband and our two boys, "Our house is a pit! I'm cleaning today." On many occasions, during my cleaning routine, my youngest son would ask if we were having company later that day. When I shared with him that we weren't having company, he would look at me with a puzzled look and ask, "Then why are you cleaning?"

"To have a clean house," I would respond.

Second, my family has always loved to travel. When my husband and I first met many years ago, we traveled frequently. Regardless whether our travels took us to Florida, Mexico, Aruba, the Bahamas, varied Caribbean islands, or exploring New England together on weekend getaways, we loved to travel as a young couple. We still love to travel.

I often joke that our passport stamps ended in 1997 with the birth of our oldest son. It's somewhat of a half-truth because on the one hand, once our children were born, our trips were not as frequent. However, we have been able to take family vacations at least once a year for as long as I can remember.

Time passes quickly. I often feel like I blinked, and my two beautiful baby boys grew up into wonderful young men overnight. Having young adult children is very often what I refer to as bittersweet. On the one hand, I miss the pitter-patter of little feet in the house. I miss the days of washing small polo shirts. I miss wiping tiny handprints from our sliding glass patio door, and I miss removing toys from the kitchen table. I miss the days of staying up until midnight and washing baseball uniforms at crazy hours only because we learned late in the evening that our sons' baseball teams had advanced to the next round of a tournament and we needed to be back at the field by 8:00 a.m. the following morning. I miss the chaos!

On the flip side, my husband and I have worked very well in tandem throughout the years. We make a good team, and it certainly is a wonderful feeling to have to pick up only for ourselves. There is less laundry to wash, less dirty plates to stack in the dishwasher, and less ink pens to search for in the pockets of teenagers' jeans. Our now spare bedrooms and guest bathroom remain cleaner for a longer period of time by virtue of little use.

Outside of our beloved cat Penny shedding her long black hair all over the place and occasionally dragging a bug or a small lizard inside as a sign of her household contribution, our house is very tidy these days.

So . . . how do people like us get bedbugs?

Believe it or not, many people get bedbugs. Statistically, Ohio, Indiana, and Michigan are the top three states with the worst bedbug problems.[1] For people who travel domestically or internationally, there is an increased risk of unwillingly bringing these nuisance pests into their homes.

I wrote each of the following chapters with the professional salesperson in mind, and I've provided sales tips and strategies that will help you be successful regardless of your product or service offering. Each chapter also addresses why one company in particular, Bed Bug Pros of Florida, won our business. My hope is that my readers can learn from our ordeal while reducing their chances of crossing paths with bedbugs.

Viewing "sales strategies" and "reducing the risk of acquiring bedbugs" in the same sentence may initially look odd; however, please trust that it isn't as strange as you may think. As you read through each chapter, the connectivity of these two phrases will become clear.

CHAPTER 1

Planning Is Important

I am currently the national sales manager for a large global manufacturer of medical hygiene products. Each year, our company hosts one of the largest long-term care conferences, with more than one thousand people from around the world attending. This educational conference is held in Poland, which is where our corporate headquarters is located.

In America, we also host an annual sales meeting for our small USA sales team to attend and collaborate with one another for a few days. We discuss sales strategies, sales challenges, industry best practices, and marketing information. This annual sales conference is also a way for our leadership team to thank each salesperson for being a valued member of our sales team.

Our most recent sales meeting was held in the month of February in the great city of Orlando,

Florida. Two of our colleagues from overseas who work in our German and Poland markets were also invited to attend our USA annual sales meeting. We had agreed that it would be mutually beneficial for all parties to have both domestic employees at the meeting as well as some teammates from abroad.

For anyone who has ever planned a sales meeting for a group, my hunch is that you can easily understand the stress that comes along with the event coordination. Navigating the planning process, which includes determining the location of the event, arranging travel schedules for those flying in from varied parts of the country, figuring out meals each day, deciding on entertainment, selecting sales content for the meeting, printing necessary sales and marketing materials, and examining related costs versus budget, is an undertaking. Every detail must be addressed to ensure a successful sales meeting. This can be compared to planning a wedding, with the big difference being that the sales meeting typically has less lead time.

Planning a sales meeting is never a one-person show. It takes many people to exchange ideas, brainstorm, and collaboratively pay attention to the smallest of details. As the person leading this past year's sales meeting, I felt confident that I had all my bases covered. I was ready. I was prepared. I was excited for my teammates to come to Orlando.

Plans were made for our sales team members to meet at the selected hotel on a Monday afternoon, check in to their respective rooms, and then attend a dinner event that evening in the hotel's lobby restaurant. This was our sales meeting official "kick-off."

As our two overseas colleagues were arriving the Sunday afternoon prior to the start of our Monday sales meeting, my direct manager and I made plans to pick them up at the airport and have dinner together that Sunday evening. It was our way of getting acquainted with one another ahead of the meeting. The four of us made plans to stay Sunday night at the hotel.

Since I live in Orlando, I volunteered to pick up our two colleagues from the airport and meet my manager at the chosen local restaurant. As I left my house on Sunday afternoon, I kissed my husband goodbye and told him I would text him later to say goodnight. Off I went to the airport, excited, and arriving in plenty of time to pick up my two colleagues.

My manager was driving down from Georgia, and she called me on her way to Orlando. We confirmed that our colleagues' flights were still on time, her drive time was going along as planned, and we reiterated our plan to meet at a waterfront restaurant in Disney Springs.

My two international traveling colleague's plane arrived on time. As they exited customs, we exchanged greetings, collected their luggage from the baggage carousel, located my car in the parking garage, paid the parking attendant, and drove to the restaurant as planned. All was going smoothly without any hiccups.

As we were eating dinner together later that evening, I received a text from my husband, along with a picture of a bug.

"I'm sleeping on the couch tonight," he said. "We have bedbugs. Can you call someone tomorrow if you get a chance?"

Have you ever had a situation when you know you have a big problem with the lack of time to solve it?

I knew immediately we had a big problem. My husband is a teacher with no free time during the day to make calls. We both have our "roles," so to speak. I've always been the one who makes the doctor and dentist appointments as well as the calls to plumbers, electricians, the water department, etc. My husband has always done the cooking, the care of our pool, and the grocery shopping. He has a knack for cleaning out our garage and closets, two things I detest doing, and so we have always worked well together.

For the last week or two, my husband and I had been noticing tiny, disgusting, dark-brown bugs on our white king-size comforter. We had both started thinking they could be bedbugs. Instead, we were holding out hope that perhaps they were dust mites or fleas from our precious cat Penny, or a host of other types of bugs. Any alternative to bedbugs!

As I read the text from my husband confirming bedbugs, my heart sank. I had heard horror stories about bedbugs throughout the years. I had heard that they spread like wildfire, that they come out at night, and that they were a pain to get rid of. As I sat at the restaurant table that Sunday evening conversing with my manager and two colleagues, I did my best to remain calm and not let this disturbing news from my husband ruin the evening. After all, there was nothing I could do at that precise moment in time.

From Seller to Buyer

I knew right away, however, that I quickly was now going to be stepping into a new "buyer" role versus my comfortable role as a "seller." As soon as we got to the hotel and checked in, I dropped my luggage in the room, booted up my computer, connected to my cell phone hotspot, and began my online research into bedbugs. The first step to my solution started with googling pest control companies and looking at their websites to learn more.

SIDE NOTE SALES TIP
Remain Calm: Understand the Difference Between Marketing and Sales

Having been in sales for thirty-plus years, I strongly believe that remaining calm in situations is a learned skill. When you can remain calm, regardless of if you are a buyer or a seller, you are able to slow your thought process down and avoid having knee-jerk reactions or making rash decisions. In light of receiving a concerning text from my husband confirming bedbugs in our home, remaining calm allowed me to better manage my evening as I knew there was nothing that I could do regarding my current situation at 7:00 p.m. on a Sunday evening.

Remaining calm also helped me gather my thoughts as to the next steps and how I would begin to solve this problem. My first task was researching and locating a company to rid our house of bedbugs. I had a very short deadline while also managing the demands of running the annual sales meeting. I knew that I had limited free time over the next few days to work on this unexpected new project and would need to multitask.

Where do I begin and how do I tackle something that I know so little about? I asked myself. I was now on the other side of the fence—from being the seller to being the buyer.

Whether you're a buyer or a seller, it is important to understand the difference between marketing and sales.

I once interviewed for an outside sales role, and the interviewer asked me to define this difference. My response went something like this: We are all marketers and salespeople at some level and in some capacity, beginning in early childhood. Marketing is creating brand awareness about a product or service. If marketing is done well, a brand will be top of mind when a need arises.

Sales is taking a deeper dive to guide prospects to buy a particular product or service based on persuasion. A skilled salesperson will provide education to the prospect, and in turn, the prospect will process the information shared, find value in that information, and thus transition from a prospect to a buyer. A sale is made when a product or service offering fills a void for a buyer.

As one example, let's assume that a husband and wife, the parents of two young boys, have just finished playing Saturday afternoon baseball games at the city ball field. After the car is repacked with the baseball bags, cleats, and now-empty water bottles, the topic of lunch comes up.

"Can we go to McDonald's?" the youngest boy, John, asks from the back seat of the car.

"I don't want to go to McDonald's," Dad says.

"What about Burger King instead?" John asks.

Mom then jumps into the conversation by stating she would prefer to go to Wendy's. Lastly, the oldest son offers his suggestion of wanting to go to Arby's because they've "got the meat."

This family conversation is an example of what brand awareness looks like. Mom, Dad, and their two boys are very aware of all four restaurant choices being presented. McDonald's, Burger King, Wendy's and Arby's all have done a solid job creating brand awareness. All four companies were top of mind for this family when they were thinking about lunch options. It's an example of great marketing for all four fast food restaurants respectively.

The conversation continues with the family now making their individual cases for each of their preferred lunch spots.

"McDonalds' has way better burgers than Arby's. Plus, we can get the thick shakes," says John as he shifts his body toward the middle of the four occupied seats to plead his case.

"Yeah, but if we go to Burger King, you can get a bigger burger, and remember how you liked their new chocolate shake last time?" says Dad.

The oldest son then adds his two cents by saying with confidence, "If we go to Arby's, we can get the five-dollar meal and save you money, Dad."

Dad then asks Mom, "Didn't you take out the hamburger meat to thaw last night? I just remembered."

"You know what? You're right. I forgot about that. We have hamburgers at home. If we don't eat them today, the meat will go bad. Let's just go home and put some burgers on the grill. It will be cheaper and easier too," Mom says.

The decision is made and confirmed by Dad. In the end, Mom turns out to be the decision maker. This is an example of sales, with all four people acting in some capacity as a salesperson. Think about it this way:

What's the need or pain point? *In this example, the need is for lunch.*

What solutions are offered? *Four different restaurant options: McDonald's, Burger King, Wendy's, and Arby's—plus an "outside-the-box" option of grilling burgers at home.*

What are some features and benefits? *Thick shakes at McDonald's, bigger burgers at Burger King, five-dollar meals at Arby's.*

Who ultimately is the decision maker? *In this example, it's Mom. Dad is the influencer.*

Sales often start at a very young age, and while the above example would be considered informal sales, understanding the difference between marketing and sales is the foundation to being successful in a professional sales role.

CHAPTER 2

Pick Up the Phone

The process of locating a pest control company to treat bedbugs wasn't easy. It was already late when I got back from my Sunday night dinner with my colleagues. I did some internet research about pest control companies to better educate myself about bedbugs. My plan was to write down some pest control company phone numbers and make outbound calls during my limited break times on Monday.

Prior to the arrival of the start of our planned Monday evening sales meeting company dinner, I had already committed to showing our two overseas colleagues the lay of the land in Orlando. We had appointments scheduled to visit senior living communities and home medical supply stores.

I had limited time to show them all I could, which basically left no time to make phone calls to pest control companies. I again did my best to remain calm, but this was a stressful time.

I learned during my internet research that there were basically two options for treating bedbugs:

- the more traditional spraying option
- thermal heat option

From what I read on the internet that Sunday evening, the thermal heat option has a higher success rate, but it also comes with a higher cost. I made screenshots of four company websites advertising that they were experts in the removal of bedbugs. Two companies advertised that they were responsive and customer-focused. Reading this verbiage was important to me; my time was limited and I needed a responsive company. Their websites, in a sense, were their current marketing arms, especially during off hours.

My husband and I spoke briefly early Monday morning. He had had a terrible night's sleep on the couch, and he reiterated that he knew for sure we had a bedbug problem. As I had mentioned earlier, we had noticed over the course of the last few weeks one, two, or three tiny little bugs, almost "flea-like," that appeared randomly on our white comforter. We thought maybe our cat brought them into our house or they were nothing more than the occasional bugs that periodically show up in our home on occasion—just part of life in Florida!

Our concern grew as the days passed, though. We noticed that when we came into our bedroom at night and turned the light on, the number of tiny bugs on our comforter were seen more frequently. Instead of one, two, or three bugs, there were now two, four, or six bugs. They were growing in small numbers—and even more disturbing was that they were showing up more consistently!

My Monday morning went as planned and during the lunch hour, I was finally able to excuse myself from my group for a few minutes to make some calls. I began to reach out to the four companies I researched the night before.

My first two calls to two different pest control companies resulted in me leaving two voicemails. I found this to be extremely aggravating. It was 1:00 p.m. on a Monday afternoon and I had limited time.

How can you advertise your company as responsive and focused on customer service, but not pick up the phone? I thought to myself. It was disheartening to be "zero for two" right out of the gate in my success rate to reach a live person.

There's nothing worse than having a major problem on your hands and needing immediate answers only to hear a voice recording on the other end asking you to leave a message. In these two cases, I did leave my name and number. And I never heard back from either one of them.

SIDE NOTE SALES TIP
Answering the Phone Helps to Develop Buyer Trust

Regardless of the industry, if you are trying to sell something that alleviates your targeted buyer's stress, and you know that there is a sense of urgency component for your targeted audience related to your product or service, it is imperative to have a human answer the phone. Doctors' offices, dental offices, funeral homes, plumbers, utility companies, etc., are some examples where chances are the person calling on the phone has an immediate problem and is seeking answers to help find a solution.

With advancements in technology over the years, I think a large number of companies have made a big mistake in replacing receptionists with voicemail machines requesting callers' names and numbers. While one may think that there is a cost savings realized, my hunch is that potential lost sales from new buyers who have an immediate need for a company's product or service are lost due to voicemail. It's not possible to develop any sort of trust with a machine, while trust can be developed quickly when we speak to a real person.

I recently had a flight canceled by a major airline. When I called to reschedule, I had to listen to a prerecorded response telling me my wait time would be eight hours, thirty-two minutes, if I wanted to speak with a customer service agent. How much trust do you think I have for this airline because of that experience?

The company I currently work for has a person in our office that picks up the phone when someone calls. We have not only acquired a significant number of new accounts from talking with our prospects, but we've also had many testimonials and referrals because we are perceived as an organization that cares about people.

While I understand that professional salespeople cannot answer every incoming call, if you can't immediately pick up the phone, I would encourage you to return the call as soon as possible.

There's a reason the saying "the early bird gets the worm" emphasizes the importance of being the first to start something. Did you know this English idiom originated in 1605?[2] The definition behind it is that birds who wake up the earliest are the birds who are more likely to be successful in finding worms for breakfast. This saying still reigns true today. Successful salespeople are organized. They have prepared ahead for the upcoming day. They pick up the phone and respond to voicemails quickly.

What would your prospects and customers say about your response time if asked?

Have you thought about ways to rearrange your daily workflow to be able to respond more quickly to your prospects?

CHAPTER 3

The Right Amount of Information at the Right Time

The third pest control company I reached out to did answer the phone. I was pleasantly surprised and instantly relieved that I had found a person to listen to me. I had newfound hope that this company could help me. The woman's voice on the other end of the line was pleasant and calming to me, and that alone decreased my inner stress. I explained my situation and shared with her that I wanted to learn about three things:

- The cost to treat bedbugs
- How their company treated bedbugs
- How soon they could come to our house

I learned a lot from speaking with this lady. She shared that of the two ways to treat bedbugs, her company only offered the chemical treatment option because they didn't have the necessary trucks and equipment to provide the thermal heat process. She also explained that the thermal heat process was a much better option, and confided that she had continuously discussed with her company owners her desire for them to get the specific equipment to be able to offer that process.

She also explained that regardless of how bedbugs are treated, my husband and I would need to do a significant amount of prep work prior to our house being treated. While the information she provided about the prep work was extremely valuable, I had no sense of how much work was involved. My momentary feeling of relief was now transitioning to stress and worry as the tone of this woman's voice began to change from a calming voice to what now sounded like the voice of a drill sergeant.

In a hurried tone, she started listing everything we would need to do prior to treatment. We would need to strip our bedsheets from each of our three beds in our house. We would have to wash all of our sheets, pillowcases, blankets, and comforters. She explained that bedbugs die with heat, and that's why the preparation process included washing most of what we owned in terms of linens. Everything would need to be dried on the hottest cycle our dryer allowed. She further shared that all the items should be placed in containers or large trash bags for temporary storage of two weeks. This process was critical to a successful outcome, she said.

She went on to say that the containers should be stored in a very hot area to reduce our risk of even one bedbug surviving. Because we live in Florida with year-round warm temperatures, the trunks and inside of our cars, along with a self-storage unit were potential storage options.

It didn't end there, though. She told me all the clothes in every dresser would need to be washed, dried, placed in sealed containers, and removed from our house too. Picture frames would have to come off every wall. Anything plugged into an electrical outlet should be unplugged, and she advised that we should unscrew the outlet plate covers from every wall.

"Bed bugs hide in outlets," she told me.

When this woman came up for air after completely overwhelming me with more stress related to the prep work that would need to be done, I asked if the clothes in our closets along with the miscellaneous items in our linen closets needed to come out as well. She replied that she recommended removing everything from all closets, following the same process as with all the other items.

My stress level had reached a new high! I had no time. My husband had no time. It also dawned on me after we hung up that we never even discussed the cost during this twenty-minute call. As I went back to the restaurant table to rejoin my colleagues, I couldn't help but feel overwhelmed as I digested the information shared with me on my recent call.

 **SIDE NOTE SALES TIP**
Do Not Overwhelm Your Prospect:
Bite-Size Pieces of Information Are
Better

Do not overwhelm your potential buyer. Sometimes too much information all at once to a potential buyer is quite simply too much! It's crucial in sales to walk in the shoes of others and always be thinking, *What is the value of my product or service offering for this person?*

It's also crucial in sales to convey messaging that engages your prospect so they want to hear more. The tone of your voice and the value of your offering either will have your prospect wanting to learn more or wanting you to go away.

Regarding my phone experience as outlined above, I was so overwhelmed after hearing about all the necessary prep work that the only thing I was thinking about was how much work needed to be done on the part of my husband and myself. I wasn't hearing "value" from the person on the phone. I wasn't hearing "what's in it for me?"

The word *help* goes a long way in sales. Some of you may recall being in kindergarten or first grade and your teacher asking your class for a "helper." Think about how many kids in that classroom raised their hands to help. Most people like to help. Biologists have determined that humans have a natural willingness to help one another.

The desire to help starts young and continues throughout adulthood. In sales, think about messaging phrases like "Our company is here to help you every step of the way," or "I know this is a lot of information to digest, but I am here to help you."

These phrases can apply to all product and service offerings, regardless of one's industry. Had the woman on the phone shared with me that there is a lot involved regarding prep work, but their company was ready to guide my husband and I every step of the way and she would email me a "to do" list regarding the prep, I certainly would have hung up the phone more at ease and in a better frame of mind. Bite-size pieces of information help to continue conversations.

The same principles hold true for those in sales

who are prospecting by phone or email, or for those who have preset meetings in person. Don't overwhelm your prospects, but instead provide them with just enough information that a two-way conversation between buyer and seller takes place.

Whether at home or at work, we've all experienced answering our phones only to have the person on the other end introduce themselves briefly and launch into their sales pitch. Our minds haven't even processed who we're talking to, and the seller has already moved steps ahead of us by tossing information our way.

So, when making phone calls to prospects, think about your objective ahead of your call. Is your objective to make a sale immediately or to obtain more time with your prospect? Instead of fast-forwarding to all the reasons you've called, how about starting with one?

For example, a sentence that starts with "Hi, Mary, I didn't mean to catch you off guard" helps the person on the other end breathe, so to speak, as you are acknowledging that they were not expecting your phone call. This one tweak to an outbound call may help to initiate a conversation.

If you are a salesperson who is making cold calls in person to prospects, think about ways to pivot a conversation first. For example, my company sells personal care products to home medical supply stores. If I open the store door, head straight to the person standing behind the register, and start spewing information about my products, that person more often than not will look like a deer in headlights, their eyes glazed and not digesting what I am trying to convey.

Rewind that same scenario and think about what may happen if I enter the store, head to one of the aisles, and just momentarily observe the store. Often, the person behind the register will leave their post, enter the aisle I'm in, and ask me if I need their help. The situation changes to a more even playing field in this scenario. The key is to then engage the potential buyer with bite-size pieces of information.

What types of information resources do you use currently to convey information to potential buyers?

What may be some new ways to share micro information with your prospects?

CHAPTER 4

Developing Trust

We made the decision to work with Bed Bug Pros of Florida even though they were initially the highest cost out of all the companies we received price quotes from. We chose them based on what we felt was their overall value to us. The words *to us* are so critical to the buying and selling process, regardless of what product or service is under consideration. A successful salesperson will always understand the phrase "What's in it for them?" versus "What's in it for me?" When you place your prospective buyer's needs and wants ahead of your own desire to make a sale, your chances of making the sale will increase.

Our primary reason in choosing this company was that their owner did an awesome job to build trust quickly with us, which led to my husband and I feeling comfortable that our nightmare could be solved. As an example, after a short phone conversation with the company owner, Scott, he advised us that it would make the most sense for his colleague to come to our home and evaluate our situation. Scott told us that his colleague Larry would visit me the following morning.

For people that find themselves in a situation where time is of the essence, "overall value" can be defined many ways. In our situation, a quick response time contributed to overall value. Scott said that Larry would come by at 11:00 a.m., and at 10:55 a.m., our doorbell rang.

First impressions matter in sales. Larry was very pleasant. His clothes were clean. He smiled when he greeted me and introduced himself. As he entered our house, he asked me about the bedbugs. I explained to Larry that we had saved two of them in two separate small clear plastic bags. When I showed him the two bags—one with a dead bug and one with a bug still moving, he confirmed that these were bedbugs.

Although I had hoped for better news, it was at this precise moment in time that Larry began to win our business by virtue of his extensive knowledge. He shared this information a little at a time. I was able to easily digest and process what he shared, as his calmness in presenting this disturbing news was helping me to better cope.

With a soothing and confident voice, Larry shared

that one of the bedbugs was a young teen bug and the other bedbug was a child. Larry told me he was fascinated with these types of bugs, how their colonies started, where they started, how they live, and where they live. He explained that current research was being done at many prestigious universities nationwide because of the unique way that these bugs form colonies.

Company credibility, quick response time, and creating a level of trust were the core factors why we chose Bed Bug Pros of Florida. We valued these things more than the cost.

SIDE NOTE SALES TIP
Sell Overall Value versus Cost

Being able to sell overall value versus cost is a learned skill set that comes in time with sales experience. It requires a salesperson to connect the dots for the buyer so the buyer understands the value of the product or service being offered. In a sense, the physical product or service offered is really the conduit to an outcome that the buyer is recognizing.

For example, I know very little about car tires, but

I think I could sell a lot of tires to people—and not just the lowest cost tires, either. I think I could sell a very high-priced tire. I don't think I would have been as confident early in my sales career to make such a statement; however, feeling confident in your sales ability greatly ties into being able to convey overall value to prospective buyers. Confidence in sales has to do with being able to understand the type of sale, the type of buyer, and the workflow, and then take all of that learned knowledge to pivot conversations.

The tire business is very much a transactional business. Whenever I have needed tires over the years, I would make a call to a tire place, share the size of my tires, provide the make and model of my car, and the person on the other end of the phone would give me a price. Maybe, on a rare occasion, the tire store salesperson would tell me that the price he just quoted me also includes a 30,000, 40,000, or 50,000-mile warranty. This information has always meant very little to me because the "why" behind the warranty—the overall value—has never been explained to me.

I have also physically visited many tire shops over the years to get pricing on tires. The sales process is not too different in person. The tire store salesperson will ask me for the same information as I would have been asked had I been on the phone. Maybe, on a rare occasion, the only slight difference is that the tire store salesperson may show me the physical tire and reiterate the mile warranty verbiage while he touches the tire tread with his fingers. Overall, this transactional sales process is about the same whether on the phone or in person.

As a career salesperson who has put miles and miles on many cars' odometers, I have spent my fair share of time in various automotive places. I have spent many hours in the waiting rooms of these places using their table and a chair as my makeshift home office for a day or more, while waiting on a repair or for new tires to be installed. I have also seen many parents come into these places to inquire about tires for their teenagers' cars or their elderly parents' cars.

I'm reminded of the days when my two boys were young teenagers driving. I remember going with them to buy new tires. I remember being worried about them driving in general, especially when they first started. I worried about other drivers hitting them. I worried about them hitting other drivers. I worried about late night storms, drunk drivers, and sleepy semitruck drivers. I also worried about their car breaking down, with many ugly "what if?" scenarios and irrational thoughts.

Now, think about a conversation taking place between a tire store salesperson and a parent, with the salesperson using the physical tire as a conduit to a favorable outcome of " less worry" for a parent. The conversation might sound something like this:

Mom: "Hello, my son has a Buick Skylark, and we would like to get some new tires, please."

Tire Salesperson: "How old is your son?"

Mom: "He is sixteen."

Tire Salesperson: "How long has he been driving?"

Mom: "He just started, maybe three months or so."

Tire Salesperson: "I'm curious, do you worry about the wet roads, especially at night?"

Mom: "Of course, I am filled with worry."

Tire Salesperson: "Well, we have three different types of tires–think in terms of good, better, best. Our best tires will help reduce the risk of the car skidding on wet pavement. They also work so well that if your son had to shift lanes quickly, the risk of his car swerving into another lane is reduced because these tires are high- performing. Basically, they will help keep your son safer on the roads."

In this example, cost is never brought up initially, and the tire is serving as the conduit to reducing risk for this mom's son, ultimately leading to less worry for her. My point is that when you can sell value, cost becomes secondary.

How do you build trust for your potential prospects?

How do you sell overall value?

How might you convert a transactional sale to a relationship sale?

CHAPTER 5

Become an Industry Expert

Larry explained to me that bedbugs don't jump, nor do they fly.

"They like to catch a ride on something," Larry explained. He told me that a female bedbug will change into a male bedbug if no males are present to mate with the female. Larry also told me that bedbugs will only grow their colonies to a certain number of bugs, ensuring that each colony member has enough to eat.

Bedbugs feed on human blood. They typically come out at night, crawl on humans, and bite. Sometimes a person might see red, rash-like bites, while other times, these aren't noticeable. After their bloody meal, these disgusting creatures return "home," which often is unfortunately a mattress or crevice within an adjustable bed. In our case, our adjustable bed platform was their home.

The more information that Larry shared with me, the more I could hear and see the passion he had for his work. His industry expertise was evident, and I found myself becoming less worried about my current situation. The more I witnessed his fascination with all things bedbugs, the more interested I was in learning even more from him. Larry's excitement about this group of insects transferred over to me, and I lost my sense of being overwhelmed by this ordeal and instead had a sense of repose, knowing that "this too shall pass."

I asked Larry how long he had been with his company treating bedbugs, and he told me seven years. He also told me that bedbugs were the only type of bugs he worked with. He went on to say that he had a 96 percent success rate exterminating bedbugs on the first try.

Larry asked if I could take him on a tour of our rooms. I started with our master bedroom since that was the only place we had seen the bedbugs. Larry held a small flashlight as he walked into our bedroom. He started shining the flashlight under the bed, up at the ceilings, at our walls, behind our television that was hung on the wall, and on top and below our dressers. I explained to him that we had been seeing four or five bugs on our white comforter for the last few weeks at night.

"One bedbug is one too many," I told him.

I was curious how common bedbugs were and how our situation compared with other scenarios he had seen. I found it interesting when Larry told me that Florida wasn't even in the top ten states where bedbugs are most common. Ohio, he said, is number one. Larry also told me about a two-inch-thick coating of bedbugs on the entire ceiling of one of the houses he had treated. He said the owners tried for five years to control the bugs themselves before calling his company.

Bedbugs were eradicated in the United States about forty years ago, but when international travel started to become more common, bedbugs began to infiltrate our country again. I learned from Larry that bedbugs initially were thought to have originated in Europe. The stigma tied to bedbugs that they are only found in dirty homes originated when they were found in the beds of brothels in Europe, "where people shouldn't be," Larry told me. I was fascinated as I had no prior knowledge about any of what he was sharing with me. On the flip side, why would I, right?

He also informed me that many flights on a major airline had been shut down not that long ago because the luggage cargo area was infested with bedbugs. Think about that for a minute. As travelers, and by no fault of our own, if our luggage is in the wrong place at the wrong time, unknowingly we can take bedbugs home with us. When I shared my ordeal with one of my co-workers, they wondered if using hard luggage versus soft makes a difference. I learned from Larry that it makes no difference at all.

"They find their way in," he said.

SIDE NOTE SALES TIP
Establishing Credibility in Sales

Establishing credibility for any business takes time and typically doesn't happen overnight. The same is true for salespeople. It's a process. However, the more you take the time to invest in learning about the product or service you are selling and the more you can learn about your industry, the more likely you will be viewed as an expert by your prospects and peers.

Many years ago, I sold endoscopes. As mandated by the company, I attended a weeklong training in their corporate offices to learn about this high-tech medical equipment. After the training, I went out into the field and attempted selling the scopes. I simply completed my training and began knocking on doors, nothing more. I didn't invest in my own learning about the industry.

A large part of my role required setting up demos with gastroenterologists to trial the endoscopes. While I could set the demos up easily, I didn't know enough to be credible. I was in the surgery suite during the procedures and always felt out of place. I had little to contribute to the conversation with the doctors and nursing care staff.

In my two-year tenure with this company, I never felt confident selling the scopes, and I have no doubt it showed. The company was a decent company to work for, and they treated me well. I don't blame them for my lack of confidence; rather, I blame myself. You see, I was the one who never took the time to learn the industry, reach out to others within my own company who had vast industry experience, or connect with other industry professionals to learn more.

It's difficult to become comfortable in a sales role if you don't take the time to learn about the industry you're in. Becoming successful as a salesperson is twofold. While it is crucial to know everything about the product or service that you are selling, becoming credible happens when you also are educated about the industry in which you are working. Merging these two concepts separate the average salesperson from the expert.

Third-party credibility can also be beneficial in

sales. The more connections a salesperson has with other like-minded industry related professionals, the more mutually beneficial ways there are to work with one another. I often think of an outside sales role as similar to sharing common ground with those who were very involved while attending middle school or high school during their teenage years. While a person may choose to spend their days simply attending classes—i.e., "knocking on doors for prospects"—those who incorporate extracurricular activities into their day are likely to be viewed as more credible due their involvement. Engagement goes a long way in sales.

Think about attending industry networking events, participating in webinars, podcasts, blog writing, co-marketing with an industry partner, and so on to help with third-party credibility. The secret is to make sure the people you are connecting with are credible themselves. Otherwise, you risk losing your own credibility.

What fulfills you in your current sales role?

What type of additional sales activities can you incorporate into your current sales role that would be beneficial to establishing third-party credibility?

CHAPTER 6

Why Transparency and Setting Expectations Are Important

The company we chose to treat our bedbug problem did a wonderful job from start to finish. A contributing factor to their success can be tied back to them being transparent from my initial phone call, and setting expectations throughout the entire sales cycle. They set expectations early in our conversation, letting me know what their services included, while also emphasizing to me the importance of my husband and I doing the necessary prep work on our end before their arrival. If we were to achieve a successful outcome, the owner shared, we would have to work together.

If you think about expectations, there are many of them—some subtle, while others are in writing—that take place between the buyer and seller during a full sales cycle. In our case, the first expectation came from me, the buyer, when I picked up the phone and called this company. My expectation was that someone from their company would answer.

After my conversation with the company owner, I had a second expectation: that the owner's colleague would arrive at my house the following morning at 11:00 a.m. as promised. I'm sure the company owner, without thinking much about it, also expected me to be at my home to greet his colleague. In this example, there are three expectations, without any of them being written. These expectations help to build mutual trust.

When Larry showed up at my house the next morning, he explained the process of his home inspection before he began. As Larry walked from room to room, he began to set expectations regarding the prep work.

For example, as we entered one of the bedrooms, Larry explained that the mattresses should be stripped of all linens and mattress covers, and then tipped on their sides. He asked me if he could lift the mattress on its side to not only look for bedbugs, but also to show me the precise way the mattress should be tipped during our prep work. After politely asking, "May I?" Larry pointed to a dresser drawer in our spare bedroom and opened the drawer, again searching for bedbugs while also explaining that the clothes would need to come out and each drawer should be removed from the dresser.

Shining his flashlight on a stack of old papers sitting on a small nightstand, he told me we should go through all our papers as bedbugs like to hide in them.

"They like old papers," he said.

I cringed, thinking about the stacks of paper sitting on top of my home office desk.

Room by room, Larry examined every nook and cranny. While my husband and I had only seen bedbugs in our bedroom, which is located on the opposite side of the house from our additional bedrooms, I was shocked to see Larry shine his flashlight at the top corner of our hallway wall and exclaim, "There's one right there," he said.

"Oh great," I responded. My heart sank with the realization that these bugs were not only in our master bedroom but throughout our entire house.

"They like to move," Larry said as he continued examining our hallway closet, additional bedrooms, and my office.

Larry spent about an hour inspecting our house. When he was finished, he shared with me that they could definitely treat them and he would have the owner reach out to me with a price. He told me not to quote him, but he thought the cost would be around two thousand dollars. This is another example of setting an expectation.

Larry also explained their thermal heat process,

which would take all day from morning until early evening. We would have to leave the house because the heat is too intense to stay inside. Our cat couldn't stay in our house during the treatment either. Larry told me the owner would be in touch, and said he would check the schedule but thought they could do the job the following week.

Within minutes of Larry leaving, I called the company owner and left a voicemail. I expressed my interest in moving forward, requested a quote, and asked for a start date. Based on the trust we'd developed and feeling confident that they would rid us of bedbugs, I was already sold. It wasn't more than five minutes after I left my voicemail that I received a text from the company owner.

Text from Bed Bug Pros of Florida owner (February 2023)

It's $1,950 to do our proven process on a home that size. We have to do an 8-10 hour thermal heat treatment process guaranteed to eradicate ALL BEDBUGS in the entire home in just one treatment. We also administer a nontoxic residual product in conjunction with the heat.
Includes our full six-month EXTENDED WARRANTY/ GUARANTEE on the entire home.

We are called Bed Bug Pros for a reason.
Licensed. Insured. Bonded.
More than thirty years' experience.
We carry the highest certification with the State
of Florida Agricultural Department.

Thank You!
Scott, owner, Bed Bug Pros of Florida

Twelve-month extended insurance
available for only $350
Prep is very critical to the success of treatment.

Prep guidelines:
- No prep necessary in kitchen, bathrooms, or closets
- Strip all beds
- Wash and dry all bedding and remove from room
- Run clothes from dressers through dryer on high for forty-five minutes
- Bag up clothes and remove from room until after the treatment.
- Clean out underneath bed
- Pick up loose clutter
- Remove candles and oil paintings

- Electronics are fine
- Can leave clothes hanging in closets
- Try to organize shoes in closets so not piled up
- Clean off dressers, nightstands, etc.
- Remove all guns and ammo unless in fireproof safe
- Pack up medications and take with you
- Plan to be out of home from 9:00 a.m. to 5:00 p.m. on day of treatment

SIDE NOTE SALES TIP
Hold Your Prospect's Hand

If you approach each sales opportunity from the mindset that you will be available to "hold your prospects hand," figuratively speaking, throughout the entire sales cycle, you will increase your chances of making more sales and having more meaningful relationships. We are social beings by nature, and relationships matter.

Establishing trust can be developed early in the sales process by following a few simple steps. For example, if you set a meeting time of 9:00 a.m. to meet with a new prospect, make sure you do everything in your power to be there no later than 9:00 a.m. While being on time may seem like such a trivial thing, showing up on time is important as this is the first step in meeting an initial expectation.

While you will not always be able to set early morning meetings, the earlier in the morning that a first-time meeting can be set, the less risk there is for other things that may happen throughout the day, thus causing you to be late.

When I think of early morning meetings, I sometimes remember how often many of us have interviewed for new sales roles. If we have lined up an interview for Monday at 9:00 a.m., for example, we more than likely know on Sunday evening by 6:00 p.m. what we will be wearing to that interview. To take it a step further, many of us in sales will have tried the outfit on even earlier than Sunday evening. We will have checked to make sure our interview outfit fits, the buttons button, and the zippers zip. Many of us will make sure on Sunday that we have plenty of gas in our car so as to not have to stop along the way. If we are unfamiliar with the address where the interview is taking place, we may even take a ride a few days ahead to ensure we know where we are going on that Monday morning. The more important the potential new role is for us, the more prepared we will be.

Think about these things for a minute. When we want the sales role, we do a lot of pre-prep to increase our chances of being offered the new role. Yet, unfortunately, when we have secured the role, we can allow ourselves to develop habits that hinder getting the sale. Preplanning in this interview example shares common ground with guiding your prospects through the sales cycle.

For example, once you establish a meeting time, consider adding a meeting agenda to the calendar invite as part of your preplanning process. You might also ask your prospect to bring a certain something that may be relevant to your meeting. For example, if you are selling compression socks and offer a high-performing sock that's better than most of your competitors, consider asking your prospect to bring a sock they are currently using to the meeting.

These few things start the process of hand-holding and guiding your prospects. When you have the meeting, always be thinking about next steps—in terms of when, not if. The more a prospect trusts you, the more they will allow you to guide them to the decision makers and what processes need to take place for them to purchase your product or service. They will be more apt to include you if you are "holding their hand." Two hands together form one palm, so to speak.

While I have never worked for a "perfect" company, I have worked for companies that are darn close. I'm proud to be working for a company now that is super responsive and offers a high-quality product. On the rare occasion we have any minor hiccups, we address them quickly and responsibly. On the flip side, I once worked for a company that had issue after issue after issue—so much so that I started setting expectations with my potential prospects.

"I want to share with you that we aren't perfect, and should there be some initial hiccups, please trust that I will be there to hold your hand every step of the way," I would say.

The key is to set the initial expectation, but even more critical is to follow through on your promise and help your customer every step of the way, whether you have minor hiccups with a great company, or too many hiccups with a not-so-great company. Only you can decide how many hiccups are too many hiccups for you to continue to feel comfortable selling your product or service. Your reputation is your personal brand!

What things do you do to help guide your prospects?

How do you prepare for upcoming initial meetings?

How do you guide your customers when hiccups happen?

CHAPTER 7

True Passion Resonates

Passion resonates! Once you find yours, you'll never want to let go. Larry the bug guy was uncommonly passionate about his work, and it showed from the minute I opened our front door to let him into our house. He smiled politely, greeted me, and within about two minutes, he began to share all he knew about bedbugs.

Keep in mind that this type of knowledge sharing is very different from a salesperson having a one-sided conversation during which they are talking "at" the buyer versus "with" the buyer. Larry was conversing with me, and it was apparent that he was passionate about his work by the tone of his voice, his level of confidence, and his vast knowledge.

Larry shared that he didn't start out with the intent of becoming a bug expert, treating homes and commercial buildings for bedbugs. He had another professional job working for a large company for many years. However, the older Larry got and the more tenured he became, the more disenchanted he felt in his prior role. When he started dreading Monday mornings, thinking about them on early Sunday afternoons so much so that his day off was consumed by negative thoughts, he knew he needed to find a new career path. A friend of a friend recommended that Larry reach out to Scott, the owner of the bedbug company, as Scott was hiring.

While it's difficult to describe Larry's passion, I felt like the more he shared his knowledge, the more I gained his trust. The more I gained his trust, the more that I felt that our bedbug nightmare would have a positive outcome. Larry's passion was so contagious that even I wanted to know more about bedbugs. He was a great teacher. He knew his stuff!

Can you even imagine finding your passion related to treating bedbugs? Passion is hard to describe, and it is not easy to find. I can't imagine that Larry's passion is directly related to the thermal heat treatment and chemicals used to remove bedbugs. My hunch is that the removal processes are the conduits to Larry's desire to help people. Larry likes to educate others too. He excels at being an expert in his field, and that has to be internally rewarding. After all, how many specific bedbug experts are there in Florida—and who actually starts out thinking they would like to be a bedbug expert?

SALES TIP SIDE NOTE
Passion in Sales

I have often wondered whether we find passion or if passion finds us. I'm not sure that, even after my thirty-plus years of sales experience, I can begin to answer that question because there are so many variables involved. I have many friends who are also sales professionals, and we have talked about this topic frequently. Having a great product or service to offer may not be enough. If the product is great, but you don't care for the people you work with, it's tough to find passion. If you really like the people you work with, but you don't feel comfortable or confident in the product you're selling, finding passion can also be challenging.

Passion is a very individualized concept. It's hard to describe, and it's even harder to explain how a person obtains it. People dynamics, the product or service you are selling, the "pocket of time" within which you are selling, and a host of other factors have to align ever so nicely for you to experience true passion in sales.

As a sales professional, I've spent most of my career going to work and selling some truly wonderful products and services. However, I never really had any true passion related to most of my prior roles. I'm not sure exactly what the reason was. It might have been a missing component to my overall experience in working for many of those companies, or perhaps it was timing. Yes, I did a great job, made decent money, and even won some sales awards and promotions along the way. Interestingly enough, though, I never knew I was missing "passion" until I actually found it.

When you have passion for what you are selling, not only will your customers, colleagues, and peers see it, but internally you will feel fulfilled every day. You will look at each day with more positivity and the hope that something really great is about to happen. You'll feel like you are driving the bus, so to speak, versus simply taking a seat as a passenger.

When you have passion for your work, often you'll unintentionally merge your workweek with your time off. There isn't this great separation between the two because your work feels like play. Personally, I have had just two sales roles I felt passionate about. The first was about ten years ago when I accepted a sales role with a large outpatient imaging company. I was hired as a sales manager, managing a small team of five or six outside sales representatives. My role was to motivate and inspire the members of my sales team to establish and strengthen relationships with referring doctors so if a doctor's patient needed a radiology exam, the doctor would encourage their patient to come to our imaging center.

I developed a tremendous amount of passion for this role after just a few short weeks of joining the company. I often think about what it was that I absolutely loved about this role. I was with this company for a total of five years. My first three years were wonderful, and my last two years reverted back to me dreading Monday mornings while thinking about "having to go to work" as early as mid-afternoon every Sunday.

In hindsight, the manager I reported to for my first three years played a major role in finding my passion. She was smart, approachable, and I felt supported by her. She managed with a "how can I help?" servant leadership style. I felt very comfortable sharing ideas with her. Some ideas of mine or my fellow teammates were terrific, while other ideas were not so great. However, at no time did I ever feel uncomfortable bringing an idea to the table.

I also worked with wonderful people on my sales team. While each one of us had strengths and weaknesses, we had a tremendous amount of camaraderie and affection for one another. Our work days were full of fun and engaging conversations. We offered a high-quality service as our team of radiologists were subspecialists, thus ensuring that the radiology reads were accurate for our patients. My team worked with a staff of caring, loyal, and committed individuals who went the extra mile to help our patients.

For three years, my role was awesome. My teammates and I were building our imaging brand. We were on a quest to not only meet our sales goals but surpass them. Heck, one year we even set a new Guinness World Record for having the longest line of people wearing stethoscopes. People dynamics, a high-quality service offering, and timing were the ingredients that allowed me to find my passion. I felt a daily feeling of excitement for three years in a row, regardless whether or not the day was a Monday, a Wednesday, a Saturday, or a Sunday. I felt passion—and it felt awesome!

Unfortunately, this company was owned by a venture capital group, and as the company grew closer to a sale date, changes started to take place within leadership. I knew things were changing when a member of the corporate leadership team paid me a visit and asked me to rank my sales team members from one to six in order of "best to worst." I explained that I had no "worst" and couldn't even begin to rank my team in that order because each team member made contributions to our team.

"We are a circular, collaborative team," I explained. The more this individual insisted that I rank my team, the more dismayed I became that things were changing at the top. What I loved so much about servant leadership and a "ground-up" support mentality was now changing to a top-down "do this" mentality.

My passion diminished over the next two years as major changes took place within that company. The people dynamics, the quality of our service offering, and everything I enjoyed about building something special was disappearing. I knew it was time to go, and I recall feeling extremely sad that I might never find this "feeling" again. I finally had felt passion for my work, and now it was gone.

Luckily, all experiences in life help to prepare us for new chapters. I am currently employed for a dynamic company with an incredible product and service offering. My new role requires a fair amount of travel , and the timing is just perfect as my two sons are young adults and living on their own. I couldn't have managed my hectic travel schedule if my boys were still young.

My manager has a heart of gold. She is smart and kind. Figuratively speaking, she can be found just about an inch or so above the dirt, and that's a huge compliment to her. She exemplifies servant leadership at its best with a bottom-up approach that asks, "How can I help?" We brainstorm. I feel supported. I am managing a sales team loaded with talent. We are all unique and have our strengths and weaknesses that help us learn from one another.

As with my prior company, I found my passion early on with this company, and it has only grown over the years. As I mentioned, true passion is unique. It can be hard to explain and even harder to find. For me, it has become clear that I need the people dynamics, a high-quality product to offer, and a mission that I not only support but can also contribute to. An added element that has me feeling even more excitement day to day is witnessing our end users having an improved quality of life due to our offering. If you are lucky enough to find passion in your work, grab the reins and don't let go. The feeling is one of the best!

Have you found your passion in sales?

What factors do you think contribute to finding passion?

CHAPTER 8

The Project Begins

After making the decision to go with Bed Bug Pros of Florida, a date was secured for early March, just a few days after Larry's home inspection. Even though this company was more expensive than some other options, we felt confident using them and felt they had the most effective treatment option.

With only a limited number of days to pack up everything in our house in preparation for the process, my husband and I began the task of gathering our clothes and removing the bed linens from all other beds in our house except our own bed. We bought plastic containers to store our household items. We used large trash bags to store our linens. We used a combination of containers and trash bags to store our clothes, socks, and underwear. We removed pictures from our walls. We unscrewed outlet covers and left them dangling in every room. We sorted through our papers, books, and picture frames. It was a huge undertaking.

My husband and I decided to tackle this project outside of our traditional working hours. In hindsight, this was a mistake, and I would encourage others who unfortunately may find themselves in this situation someday to learn from our mistake. Take a few days off from work, and my hunch is there will be less internal pressure.

In a sense, this massive project felt very similar to those times when we had moved from one home to another when we were much younger and just starting out. The big difference was that this time we didn't have another wide-open space on the other end waiting for us. Instead, we used our outside patio lanai as a storage area for some of it. We used the inside of our cars as temporary storage. We stored some of the containers in our garage, and we rented a small self-storage unit nearby too. All of this took time. What made the feeling so overwhelming was that we knew we would have to repeat this process once the treatment was done. Bed bugs stink!

We also had to figure out what clothes we needed for the next couple of days and not pack those with our other stuff. Everything during that time felt like a big deal. People do what they need to do, though, and like anyone else, we got our side of the "expectations" completed the night before the project was scheduled to begin.

Early that following morning, we moved our cat Penny outside to our screened lanai along with her litter box, food, and water bowl. She was not happy about her new "home" and started whining by the patio door, expressing her dismay about being placed outside so early in the morning. Typically she greets me daily as I exit my bedroom door each day. We exchange our "hellos," and as part of what has become my daily routine, I refill her water bowl, replenish her cat food, place a couple of Friskies "treats for cats" on her rubber food mat, and clean out her litter box. Now her early morning routine had been disrupted.

The Debugging Begins

Larry arrived on the morning of March 1st, just before 8:00 a.m. He was once again very pleasant when he arrived, smiled politely, and asked if I would open the garage door so he could move his equipment in. We took a quick walk throughout the house, and he commented that we had done a good job with our removal task list.

Larry explained that he would start the thermal heat process in our master bedroom since that's where most of the bedbugs had been found. He would then continue to heat the remainder of the house, and his hope was that by 2:00 or 3:00 p.m., the process would be completed. He explained that we would not be able to reenter our house until probably 6:00 or 7:00 p.m. that evening to allow time for the house to cool down.

He reminded me to turn the air conditioning system off, and he advised against us turning the air conditioning back on until the house cooled down on its own. I can't recall all the details regarding why using the air conditioner to cool the house was not recommended, but I believe it had to do with the air conditioner not being able to cool down from a 130-degree temperature, causing our A/C system to work on overdrive for little gain and possible damage to the system.

I told Larry I would be outside in our lanai for the day as my work schedule was packed with a number of conference calls and a list of things to do. I gave Larry my cell phone number and asked him to text me if he needed anything. Settled in my makeshift office, I began to work, making phone calls and responding to emails.

An hour later, Larry texted me and asked if I had a minute. I came inside, walked into our bedroom, and Larry said, "Take a look—there they are." I was shocked and disgusted by what I saw.

"They have probably been there for three to five months," Larry said. I asked him how he knew, and he told me he could tell by the amount of colonies that they had made. The thought of my husband and me sleeping in the same bed with bedbugs for the past three to five months was disturbing and sickening. It was very alarming.

I appreciated the fact that Larry was so passionate about bedbugs that he never made me feel like this was uncommon or that we were dirty people. His comments were quite the opposite, in fact. He shared that we had a minor case compared to many other people for whom he provided services. After getting more of an education about bedbugs, I went back out to the lanai to continue my work and share some of what I had learned with my husband and close friends.

The beautiful thing about learning
is that no one can take it away from you.

B.B.KING

SIDE NOTE SALES TIP
Listen, Digest,
Understand, Learn

There have been numerous books and articles written about the benefits of being a lifelong learner. Improved brain health, developing a new skill set, and self-fulfillment are just a few examples. Most lifelong learners will agree that continued learning, whether structured or unstructured, provides significant value. On the flip side, some people believe that lifelong learners may spend too much time away from family and friends focused on learning.

Having spent many years surrounded by professional salespeople, I haven't met a successful salesperson yet who isn't a lifelong learner. While the learning aspect is important, I believe one must master the skill set of listening and also digesting information. When a salesperson can effectively listen, digest, and understand information their potential buyers are conveying, that's when a salesperson truly excels.

After graduating college, my very first role as a salesperson was with a startup company in the silver reclamation industry. This was before the world went digital, and the company I worked for offered a service where silver particles were recovered from film processors in X-ray departments at hospitals. "X-ray" departments eventually became "Radiology" departments, and now they are commonly known as "Diagnostic Imaging" departments.

As new rules and regulations started to become law related to how many years medical records had to be retained and stored, the company I worked for evolved into a document storage company. I was hired as a hybrid telemarketer to obtain meetings. When I secured a meeting with a hospital department head, my role was then to meet my potential buyer in person, assess their situation, and provide a quote to move the medical records from a temporary small holding area in a hospital to a larger storage location. The larger storage area was almost always located in the hospital basement. The records were stored there until they met retention requirements and then destroyed.

I always came to the in-person meetings with a notebook and a pen. My manager had instilled in me the importance of writing down every detail to ensure that I understood the details of the project and thus could provide a quote to move the records. For quite some time, I did as I was told. I had my pen. I had my notebook. I was on time. I smiled politely, introduced myself, and then began to ask some questions of my potential new client. The problem was that the conversation was rarely a back-and-forth, quality dialogue. I wasn't really listening as I was focused more on my writing to make sure I captured every detail. These projects involved measuring linear footage, measuring shelving space, counting the number of steps from one storage location to the other, accessibility to the locations, etc. We brought in barrels and carts to move the records, and so finding out where the loading dock was located, what the receiving hours were, and who the hospital contacts involved in the project were important details.

Once I left these meetings with a pile of notes in hand, all I had were words on paper, measurements on paper, and people's names on paper, but I never truly understood the project. It wasn't due to a lack of effort, preparation, or listening. The reason was that I didn't allow myself to digest the information. If a salesperson doesn't digest the information, it makes it very difficult to understand a buyer's needs, and thus the salesperson can amass a bunch of facts and figures but will have missed the much more significant concept of the "why" behind the project.

Fortunately, it wasn't too long before I started taking less notes but understanding more. I found that listening to my prospects, digesting information, and taking fewer notes actually helped me learn more about their needs.

How do you prepare for meetings with potential new clients?

What are some topics that you know very little about now but think may be interesting to explore?

What things are you working on to develop professional growth?

CHAPTER 9

The Project Continues

Finding common ground with people is actually very easy to do if you are mindful about the concept. I met Larry the bedbug guy just two times. The first time was when he came to our house to assess our bedbug situation. The second time was when he came back to our house to provide the thermal heat treatment process to rid us of the bedbugs.

While Larry was inside our house for approximately eight hours, I remained on our lanai for most of the day. I didn't spend much time with Larry, and certainly outside of bedbugs being our only connection, I wasn't looking for common ground. However, connectivity and common ground often go hand in hand.

Just before noon on the day of the thermal heat treatment, my laptop unexpectedly shut down. I had set up my makeshift work desk close enough to reach an outside power outlet. After trying to turn my computer back on with no success, I began trying additional outside outlets around the back exterior of our house. None of them worked either, and so, with my open laptop in my hands, I went around to the front of the house in search of finding power. I knew there was an outlet located inside the entryway to our front door that I could try.

I noticed Larry sitting in the back of his truck making a phone call. He hung up within a few minutes of seeing me, and I asked him if he had shut off the power. He said he didn't think so but went to check. He returned about two minutes later and apologized as he had unintentionally shut the power off to the outside electrical outlets.

Larry told me the reason he was sitting in his vehicle was that he had to wait for a few hours until our bedroom heated to 130 degrees, and it was too hot for him to be inside. He was planning to make a quick trip to do an assessment of a local nearby nursing home and said he would return in about an hour. Little did Larry know that I work for a company that manufactures adult incontinence products and one of our core markets is nursing homes.

And so, that became our "connection." I learned from Larry that many nursing homes and senior living communities unfortunately have bedbug issues. Who would have thought? While I had never even considered that notion prior to meeting Larry, it made sense to me once he said it. Quite often, when older adults move into a long-term care community, they are able to bring their own beds and their own furniture. Senior living community owners and operators want residents to feel comfortable in their new home, and so by bringing their own items with them, the hope is that a new environment will not feel so uncomfortable for people.

As a person who works in the senior living industry, I wasn't familiar with any senior living community staff members examining furniture or beds being brought into their communities from new residents moving in. *Should our industry be concerned about this?* I wondered.

My mind started racing to many scenarios that potentially carry risk with them. I started thinking about large senior living communities that may have licensure to accommodate one hundred residents or more and how many new resident move-ins take place on a monthly basis. The word *risk* continued to be on my mind as I thought about all the beds coming from different home environments merging into senior living communities. I also thought about how adult children, traveling from all over different parts of the country to assist their parents with a transition into a senior living community, might also unintentionally bring bedbugs with them.

Can you imagine being a son or daughter trying to help your mom or dad, and then unintentionally, by no fault of your own, creating a problem? Larry and I talked about the possibility, and he told me it's not that uncommon. We both concluded that it happens more than we know. Bedbugs have a stigma, and so it's not a subject people want to bring up. Often the situation is ignored until it snowballs into a much larger problem that must be addressed.

Connecting with Larry regarding his work in nursing homes was super helpful. I'm more mindful now about the risk of bedbugs not only in my personal life, but also while "on the job" when visiting senior living communities. On the off chance that the topic comes up in my professional dealings, I am definitely more well versed around this subject matter, and if someone needs help in Florida, I know exactly who to guide them to.

SIDE NOTE SALES TIP
Finding Common Ground and Connectivity

I moved from Boston to central Florida close to twenty years ago. When my husband and I moved here with our two young boys, we didn't know a soul. It was important to us to live in a neighborhood with lots of children so our boys could make some friends. It was also important to both my husband and me to live in an area with a good school system. Shortly after moving to our new neighborhood, I befriended a couple of women—one who lived around the corner from us, and one who lived down the street. The three of us were all neighborhood walkers, and we used to cross paths with one another around the same time each night.

My separate conversations with each of these two women initially started as pleasant courtesy exchanges. However, over time, I began to stop during my nightly walks and chat a little bit more with each of them. What I learned was that the three of us—Sandy, Tracy, and I—shared common ground in that we were all from the greater Boston area. I was the only one that knew this at the time because while I was making friends with each of them, they did not know each other.

As I got to know them, I began to take walks with Sandy on some nights and Tracy on other nights. Once I became friends with both of them and better understood their backgrounds, I suggested that the three of us should walk together as we shared quite a bit of common ground. We all had young children, our husbands were sports fanatics, and we all had relatives still living in the greater Boston area. We picked a night to walk together and selected a meeting spot in the neighborhood. In this role, I acted as the connector. Much to my surprise, and not in my wildest dreams, would I have thought that by the end of that first night when we walked together, our common ground would transition to the much deeper sense of connection.

Here's what happened. I introduced Sandy to Tracy, and Tracy to Sandy. Very quickly, they began to ask each other what part of Massachusetts they were from. Sandy explained that she had grown up in Marshfield. Tracy shared that while she was born and raised in another part of the state, she moved to Marshfield as a teenager. That piece of shared information led Sandy to ask Tracy what part of Marshfield she lived in. Tracy then told Sandy the neighborhood name in Marshfield, to which Sandy responded, "You're kidding me—I lived in that same neighborhood."

As they continued this back-and-forth specific neighborhood conversation, they came to realize that Sandy's parents had sold her childhood home to Tracy's parents. Even more fascinating was when Tracy told Sandy that an extraordinarily large, colorful painting had been left in the garage from the prior owners, Sandy's parents. Sandy knew exactly what picture Tracy was referring to. The conversation cemented their friendship.

My point in sharing this example is that while finding common ground helps in establishing relationships, connectivity strengthens a relationship to a much deeper level. Numerous sales- related articles and books have been written about finding common ground with your prospects. I think it's more important to find some level of connectivity. Over the course of my sales career, some of my best relationships have been formed not just from having common ground alone, but from experiencing memorable events or unique circumstances together. Connection is more sticky, so to speak, than common ground. In sales, stickiness with customers is a good thing.

What are some ways to find common ground with potential buyers?

From your viewpoint, what does connecting with customers look like?

CHAPTER 10

Follow-Up and Account Maintenance

Larry completed the thermal heat process around 3:00 p.m. Before he left, he reminded me about our follow up "to-do" list and said he had also sent a text to me as he knew the follow up information was a lot to remember.

I received the text as we were still talking. I quickly looked at his text when it came through and smiled back at his happy emoji.

It was the perfect personal touch ending to our communication, which had helped me remain calm throughout this entire ordeal. Even the tone of his text was calming. I always felt comfortable that everything would be okay.

Text from Larry, March 2023

BB job complete ☺

- Seal all mattresses and box springs. Mattresses and box springs should be sealed in mattress ENCASEMENTS (not mattress covers!!) so if there are any lingering bedbugs they die of starvation.
- Vacuum your entire home (bed frames, mattresses, box springs, all furniture make sure to get down deep in cushions)every day for four days following treatment. Then once weekly. If your vacuum cleaner requires a bag, only use disposable bags and throw it away in an outdoor garbage can immediately after vacuuming.
- Reinspect your home regularly after treatment. Don't just look in rooms that were previously affected. Inspect all adjacent rooms as well. Use a bright flashlight to look in bed frames and deep in furniture cushions.
- Thoroughly wash and clean all the surfaces in your home, especially in your kitchen and bathroom.

Larry said he felt pretty confident that he'd gotten all the bugs on this first try. However, he recommended that we buy a one-year warranty for $350. While my husband and I typically are not fans of buying warranties, we decided to buy this warranty without question. Larry told us we could renew the warranty yearly—and we will! We learned that bedbugs can live in crevices or in walls for up to a year without being seen. Then they can start reproducing again, and again, and again.

After Larry left, I spent the rest of the afternoon on the lanai. My husband came home around 5:00 p.m., and as I heard the garage door open, I finally left the lanai and went back inside. I'm not sure what I was expecting, but I didn't realize that our two sectional sofas, one located in our living room and the other in our family room, would be taken apart piece by piece. The mattresses remained tipped on their sides, and all the dresser drawers were dismantled and dispersed throughout the rooms.

Nothing had changed in our closets, although all the closet doors were wide open. Coat closets and our bedroom closets had some clothes in them as Larry had told us previously that clothes in closets on hangers could remain if they were hanging loosely. As he said, "Bed bugs don't fly."

What's funny to think about in hindsight is that

while our house looked like it had been ransacked, it was actually a relief to see that Larry had done such a detailed job. In a weird way, I think both my husband and I felt like we were finally on the other side of this nightmare.

Bed Bug Pros' follow-up was excellent across the board, from start to finish. When it comes to bedbugs, I consider Larry to be my "trusted advisor," so much so that I've added him to my cell phone contacts. No offense to Larry, but I hoped I wouldn't have to call him ever again.

While it has been close to a year since our bedbug problem was resolved, my husband and I are still on high alert. That's how much this experience has taken its toll on us.

About nine months later, I did reach out again to Larry. While my husband was in the shower one weekday morning, I got out of bed and noticed a small, disgusting, dark-brown bug on our bedroom carpet.

What the heck is that? I thought to myself. Fortunately, it was dead, but still . . .

I went to the kitchen, unplugged my charging cell phone from its cord, took a picture of the bug, and sent it to Larry. I received a response back from him within five minutes. Keep in mind, this was nine months after he'd completed work for us, and it was also an early weekday morning. Another example of great follow-up!

Actual text from me to Larry, including picture, sent December 2023

Me: Hi. This lone bug was on our bedroom carpet. Hoping not a bedbug. What do you think? We had our mattress covers with those covers you recommend after you got rid of them for us in March, I think March. No bites on us but hoping this bug is another type of bug.

Text from Larry five minutes later

Larry: Hello, this is Larry. That is not a bedbug. It looks to me to be in the roach family or more likely a beetle family kind of looks like a baby American roach not 100% sure on what species of insects it is but it's definitely not a bedbug.

 **SIDE NOTE SALES TIP**
How You
Communicate
Matters

One of the first sales books that I ever read was *The 7 Habits of Highly Successful People* by Stephen R. Covey. For those of you who have read this book, you may recall in one of the early chapters, Covey tells a story about a father who gets on a bus with his rambunctious kids. The father is not paying attention to his kids and is negatively judged by the other bus riders. If memory serves me correctly, the reader then learns that the father had just lost his wife moments earlier, and was doing all he could to process what had happened. The moral of the story was that we can have a change in mindset when we better understand all the pieces and parts of a situation. Without understanding, it is unfortunately easy to rush to judgment.

In today's world, we have many options when it comes to communicating with people. We can meet in person. We can meet virtually. We can text or email one another. We can post on social media. We can use the phone or send a letter if we should choose that route.

When it comes to salespeople connecting with

potential prospects, as a whole, today's workforce is extremely lean across the board. A large number of people are working 100 percent remote, and a significant number of other people work in hybrid roles. I'm seeing more and more email signature lines that no longer include a phone number. Couple these challenges with phone scams, text scams, and it's no wonder having an initial conversation with a new prospect is a feat in and of itself.

If you are fortunate enough to reach a potential new buyer, how you communicate with them in the first thirty seconds is critical to gaining another thirty seconds of their time. Get to your point quickly in the conversation if there is an "ask" involved and you're talking by phone. If you are reaching out by text, make sure that your "ask" is in the first two sentences. Otherwise, you may lose your prospects' attention.

During a meeting with a prospect, it's a good idea to ask them how they'd like to best communicate with you. If they answer by cell phone or text, ask them if you can exchange cell numbers right then and there. You'll be surprised how paying attention to the little things all contribute to better mutual communication. Setting an expectation with a potential buyer is okay, too, as long as the language and tone of your voice resonates positively with them. It's okay to ask them to please not ghost you or leave you stuck in the "gray."

What would your prospects say about your communication skills?

What are some methods of communication that work well for you?

What are some "outside the box" ideas to reach prospects?

CHAPTER 11

Serving as a Resource

Many years ago, I accepted a sales role for a company that made medical record file folders, court records, and a host of other paper-related products. I didn't work for them for too long, but during my short stint with this company, I learned a very valuable lesson regarding serving others in the capacity of being a resource versus thinking in terms of trying to sell someone something.

"It's a mindset thing," my sales manager told me while having dinner one night at an Italian restaurant.

I liked this manager because he spoke from the heart and had strong morals and ethics. We had a long conversation that night about people in general. He shared his high-level view about the general population, telling me how most people want the same things in life. People want to feel loved. People want to feel safe. People want to feel supported. People want to feel validated.

We had a great dialogue back and forth about what is important in life, and it was that particular conversation that helped me pivot from a "selling" mentality to a "serve others" mindset. Over the years, I have placed those four strong statements into buckets and incorporated them into my sales process.

People want to feel loved (or liked). When looking at this statement from a sales perspective, think about the hidden value of likability. I still believe in the old philosophy that "people buy from people." The more they like you, the more you increase your chances of having continued conversations. However, it's important to realize that the general public are much more educated consumers today than ever before, so it's still critical to become an expert about your product or service offering. Learn all you can about your industry and seek out resources yourself to continue to grow professionally. Likeability will not trump knowledge. Did I like Larry the bedbug guy? I did like him. He was pleasant, kind, and respectful. Ultimately, however, I was sold on the knowledge that he and his owner provided.

People want to feel safe. Concerning this statement, think more in terms of people wanting to feel comfortable with you. If your prospect is sitting in a chair when you enter their office, ask if you can sit too. Align with potential buyers physically and emotionally. Quite often in sales, there is a subtle "superior versus inferior" mindset between buyers and sellers. If you do all you can to eliminate this way of thinking for both you and your prospect, you will find yourself having more comfortable conversations. For example, when Larry and I walked from room to room while he was inspecting our home, we were aligned. I felt comfortable that we had found a solution to our bedbug problem.

People want to feel supported. Support and communication go hand in hand. Just by simply answering my phone call, the company's owner, Scott, made me feel supported right out of the gate. That type of support continued throughout the entire process because both Scott and Larry communicated with me very well. Walking prospects through a process they are unfamiliar with goes a long way to developing relationships in sales.

People want to feel validated. One of my core beliefs is that you can't tell another person how to feel. People feel how they feel, but what you can do is acknowledge a person's feelings and then provide them with knowledge so they may internally start to feel differently. As Scott and Larry shared more and more information with me about bedbugs, I began to feel less threatened by the bugs and less anxious about the situation. Rather than feeling like an outsider, I learned that having a bedbug infestation is not all that uncommon. My logic and research confirmed that pest removal companies like the one we used would not be in business without enough customers to support their business.

SIDE NOTE SALES TIP
Prospects and
Sales Perspective

A while ago, my work cell phone rang. I picked it up only to have the person on the other end thank me for answering his call. He thanked me prior to even before introducing himself. I recall thinking how uncommonly grateful he was just because I answered his call. I sensed that he was in a panicky mood. I could tell by his tone of voice that he was stressed and short on time. He explained that he had a child with special needs and was looking for a child's diaper specifically made for swimming.

He was familiar with the company I work for because we provide adult incontinence products to the same senior living community where he was employed as a physical therapist. That was our common ground and how he got my phone number. He shared that he and his wife had never taken a vacation before with their small children. While they were excited, he explained that it took a lot of preplanning on his wife's part, and he assured her that he would take a few things off of her plate, such as finding the swim diapers.

While we don't offer swim diapers for children, I was able to point him in the direction of a company that does. He expressed his gratitude for the guidance and told me he was on a short work break and trying to juggle a bunch of trip-related things that needed to be done. It was important to him not to miss a beat with his work schedule, he told me, and he also shared that his family trip meant a lot to him and his wife because they initially thought traveling would never be possible. Without him going into great detail, I could sense that their child had some challenging medical conditions. Our conversation evolved into a conversation about hope, the way we all view the world differently, what we find important, and what challenging times we are all living in.

I hung up the phone feeling inspired by this guy. While I had helped him to find a product, our conversation helped me to remember to always maintain perspective. Having perspective in a sales role is important. Having perspective about life is even more important. While professional salespeople get paid to perform, fulfilling conversations when no sale is ever made often hold tremendous value in that they promote overall well-being. Emotional well-being ultimately leads to more sales.

What options do you provide your prospects when you can't directly help them?

What are some ways that overall well-being leads to securing sales?

CHAPTER 12

Silver Linings

I'm a firm believer that for every rotten situation we may experience in life, there is always a silver lining. I believe that God gave us the ability to daydream as a coping mechanism to navigate life and deal with the many curveballs that come our way. Some curveballs only brush us, while others hit us head-on. We all view the world from a different set of lenses, and how we react to curve balls will always vary based on our individual life experiences.

While having a bedbug infestation was a horrible experience at the time, I am able to now see more clearly all the silver linings that came along as a result of that experience. One of the biggest silver linings was that the situation forced me to go through my dresser drawers, which I hadn't done for a long time. I pulled out three to four bags of clothes, some still with tags on them, that I placed in large garbage bags and took to Goodwill. As the saying goes, one person's trash is another person's treasure. My old clothes hopefully will make multiple people happy.

My husband took on the task of sorting through our two sons' old clothes that they left behind when they moved out, and we added these to our donation pile for Goodwill. I have no doubt that many young kids who became the recipients of my children's football jerseys with Tom Brady's or Rob Gronkowski's names on the back will be filled with joy for a period of time.

My husband began to play the "remember this?" game with me as he went through our kids' dresser drawers. I'd be in our kitchen, and he would show me a small shirt, an old Halloween costume, or a worn baseball cap. We'd then think back to wonderful memories of our boys' childhood. Just as much as I love having the privilege to be able to daydream, I also love having the ability to go down memory lane. Getting lost in thought is a wonderful place to be occasionally.

Another silver lining is that by the time the removal project was over, our house was the cleanest it had ever been. Another silver lining involved our mattresses. Larry recommended that we purchase mattress protectors for every bed in our house. He explained that mattress *protectors* are different from mattress *covers*.

Protectors are zippered casings that enclose the entire mattress, thus not allowing bedbugs to make a home.

Now, you may be wondering how having to buy mattress protectors is a silver lining. My short answer is that it's a mindset thing. It's a proactive approach to minimizing our risk of ever having bedbugs again. Learning from our lousy experience gave us the knowledge we needed to be proactive going forward.

Another silver lining to this bedbug problem involved dining out. For many years, our family of four was in the habit of going out to dinner on Saturday nights. Sometimes during the week, we would also go out to dinner on Friday nights. Some weeks it was one or the other, and on a rare occasion, a Thursday night dinner may have been thrown into the mix. However, we never went out for dinner on a Monday, Tuesday, or Wednesday evening. With work schedules, school schedules, baseball schedules, and so on, life was hectic when our boys were young.

Larry finished the thermal heat removal project on a Wednesday afternoon. He told us that our house would need to cool down for several hours, so my husband and I decided to go out for dinner that night. Dining at a restaurant on a Wednesday night was new territory for us. We ended up sitting at the bar within the restaurant, and that, too, was somewhat new for us. We were breaking our habits in a good way.

Fast-forward to today: my husband and I quite often now will catch a sporting event on TV at a local bar and grab dinner on a Wednesday evening. It breaks up our weekly routine. Without having bedbugs, I'm not sure we'd be eating out on a Wednesday evening. Always look for silver linings, and you will find them!

Lastly, while I will not claim to have become a bedbug expert by any means due to my experience, I have learned a lot. My positive personal experience with Bed Bug Pros of Florida has made me a champion of their company and services. You can bet that in the unfortunate situation that I have a friend, co-worker, colleague, or family member who gets bedbugs and resides in Florida, I will be recommending this company. For anyone residing outside of this company's coverage area, I can at least serve as an experienced resource to help educate other people as they navigate this unpleasant situation.

SIDE NOTE SALES TIP
Let Your Cup
Runneth Over

Unless it's a terminal illness, everything else in this world is fixable, and that's the best thing about life, in my opinion. While I am not naive, and I understand that others may think this way of thinking may sound "Pollyanna-like," the reality is that it's true. Why? Because we have options. How we choose to view the world and utilize our options is up to us.

Unfortunately, many choices often come with stress, worry, hard work, financial implications, etc. Regardless, we should be thankful we have options. Life is not easy, and many of us unintentionally get caught up in what I think of as the "black cloud." When negative things are happening in our lives, we tend to think those negative things will be ongoing. The reality is that the only constant in life is that time is moving forward; changes are happening with every ticktock on the clock. Slow changes are hard to see, and that's why the black cloud can easily stick around if we let it.

Professional sales people face rejection frequently and have a constant pressure to sell. Salespeople can get caught in the trap of thinking that nothing will change. The key to escaping the trap, whether professionally or personally, is to start each day with a reset in how you think. Years ago, I would have encouraged salespeople to have a "glass half-full" mentality. There are so many challenges today, though, that to be successful in sales, it's important to start each day from a "cup runneth over" mentality.

Day-to-day life activities, both professionally and personally, can cause small drips to leak from your cup. Thus, if you start with a "glass half-full" mentality, you may find little water in your cup by the end of the day. On the other hand, if you choose to start with a "glass runneth over" mentality, the daily drips of life will leave you with your glass being half full. It's your choice! Choose wisely, and you will sell more because people are drawn to optimistic and happy people.

Force yourself to think positively about all the wonderful things in life that currently bring you joy. Is it your family, your children, your significant other, your home, your pet? Now think about the things you enjoy doing. Do you like to run, walk, travel, golf? What would you really like about your sales role if there was never any rejection? This is where daydreaming is extremely important. Is it the preplanning, the meeting itself, or maybe the thrill of hearing the words, "We would like to move forward" from your new customer? Do you get excited about viewing your bank account when you know a large commission check is being deposited? Do you have dreams of taking a big trip, helping your kids, retiring, or traveling? Think about conversations with your prospects, customers, and co-workers. Is that the part of selling that excites you the most?

Excitement and motivation will vary from salesperson to salesperson, but the key to a successful career in sales starts with how you view your role, your offering, your company, your colleagues, your prospects, and your customers. A positive mindset is one that can see blue skies consistently.

What are three things you love about selling?

If you could remove one challenging aspect from your sales process, what would it be?

What are some ways to stay motivated each day?

CHAPTER 13

Ripple Effects

Where did we get the bedbugs in the first place? Larry thought the bedbugs had been in our house for three to five months. The thought of that is still disturbing to me. It was March 2023 when Larry shared his opinion, and so I started thinking about where we'd been during the months of October through February.

Professionally, I had a hectic travel schedule the fourth quarter of 2022. I traveled frequently by plane and spent many nights in hotel rooms. I limit my travel to two major hotel chains, but as I learned from Larry, this makes no difference. Bedbugs do not discriminate. My husband and I also took some weekend trips, and we flew to Colorado in early December. In addition, we had family members and friends visiting with us on varied weekends.

Could they have possibly brought the bedbugs with them? we wondered.

My husband and I played the "What if?" game for a little bit longer before coming to the same conclusion: It was impossible to pinpoint where we got them, how we got them, and why we got them. At the end of the day, it wouldn't make any difference to know now anyway. We had a bedbug issue, and we resolved it. We moved forward.

While I think many of us play the "What if?" game at certain times in our lives, time moves forward and so, depending on the situation, when we play this game, we'll only learn a lesson versus having a changed outcome.

Outcomes tie hand in hand with the ripple effects that happen every single day in our lives. As my girlfriends and I age, we talk about our families, our spouses, our children, our professions, etc. We probably sound like broken records as the same conversations have taken place year after year from the day we left college.

"What if you could start all over again?" one friend will frequently ask.

Our conversations may start with how we would do things differently, but we always end up with the same conclusion: none of us would choose to go back in time. Through the years, we have discussed what our lives may have looked like had we attended a much larger college with a big name football team or a NCAA basketball team. We probably would have met hundreds more people and had many more career options. Regardless, we always revert back to the same conclusion. We laugh and realize if that were the case, we would not have met one another. We tell one another, "Yeah, but if that happened, then this wouldn't have happened."

SIDE NOTE SALES TIP
Be an Opportunist

From a professional sales perspective, the more a salesperson can pivot, the more opportunity is in play for a positive outcome. Choose to see the good in ripple effects. If you look, you will find them, and that will lead to hidden sales opportunities that present themselves. Take advantage of these opportunities and keep moving forward.

Once, when I worked for the outpatient imaging company I mentioned in Chapter 7, my teammates and I decided to host an early morning breakfast with the hope that forty or fifty central Florida area physicians would attend the breakfast to learn how our subspecialty radiologists could help their patients with a host of pain management injections and procedures.

As the sales manager, I took the lead on this project and also internally took on much of the responsibility. Our keynote speaker was our vice president of operations who had rearranged her busy schedule to accommodate our event date and time. My teammates and I spent weeks developing flyers for the event, delivering those flyers to the physicians' offices, having conversations with the physicians about the event, and obtaining their commitment to attend.

Out of the almost fifty physicians that we approached, twenty-six registered for our breakfast. We were excited, as we considered getting half of our targeted audience as work well done. We continued working with the hotel and restaurant staff to make sure all the details were taken care of. We arranged for audiovisual equipment to use during the upcoming meeting. Every detail was worked out, and we felt confident we were ready for our big day. We felt strongly that once these doctors understood the key differentiator in our offering, we would surely see more of their patients become our patients too.

On the day of the event, although we had twenty-six physicians registered, only three had shown up by the breakfast start time. My heart sank as I greeted our speaker at the hotel lobby entrance to guide her to the meeting room.

"Are we ready?" she asked.

I remember feeling queasy as I shared with her that we only had three physicians. I felt like our sales team had failed. I felt like I had failed. My attitude changed almost immediately when she looked at me and said, "That's okay—we will make the meeting cozy." And we did!

As we entered the meeting room together, some of my teammates had already taken their seats and were spread out at the tables. The room looked much too big for the few people in it. Our vice president of operations asked if everyone wouldn't mind squeezing into one table so we could get to know one another. Instead of presenting her slide deck from behind a podium as we had originally planned, she instead just spoke from her heart to all of us at the table. For the next forty-five minutes, deep meaningful conversation flowed among all of us.

By the time our meeting came to an end, we had become fast friends with these three physicians, and all three became what we called high-referring physicians, meaning they trusted us enough to send their patients to us for specific procedures. In a sense, our physician team became an extension of their practice. My point in sharing this story is that in sales, you have to pivot and take advantage of every opportunity. You have to move forward versus looking backward. Had all twenty-six physicians attended this meeting, would we have developed tight relationships with all of them? We'll never know the outcome, of course, and so spending time thinking about all the "what ifs?" is time wasted. We pivoted in that moment, took advantage of the opportunity at hand, and the result was a positive ripple effect that led to a favorable outcome.

When I was young and headed to college, I had dreams of being a writer. For a host of reasons, instead I became a professional salesperson, eventually working my way up to a sales manager and currently working in the role of a national sales manager. As I mentioned in my introduction, overall I count my blessings, and I am one lucky person. I am also a grateful person. I am grateful for every sales role, every co-worker, every prospect, and every customer I have crossed paths with—the good, the bad, and even the ugly, so to speak. Everyone we cross paths with in life contributes to our lives, contributes to our pivots and our ripple effects, and contributes to new opportunity.

Had my husband and I never had a bedbug

infestation, the opportunity to write this book would not have presented itself, and for that I am extremely grateful. Throughout our entire bedbug experience from start to finish, many ripple effects have taken place, all leading to the favorable outcome of me circling back to a younger version of myself to write a book. If I can share one piece of advice that perhaps will help younger people entering the world of professional sales, that piece of advice would be, "Be an opportunist!"

What hidden opportunities are you currently working on?

How have mentors in your life contributed to your success in sales?

Proactive Checklist to Reduce Your Risk of Getting Bedbugs While Traveling

- Always place your luggage on a hotel luggage rack.
- Always inspect the mattresses in hotel rooms to see if they have mattress protectors. If they do, that is a positive sign that they are reducing their hotel guests' risk of acquiring bedbugs.
- Never bring your luggage into your bedroom when you come home from a trip. Instead, unpack in another room. Spray your empty luggage with alcohol and place it in your garage or basement for 3 days before storing it.

GOT BED BUGS?

Preparation Checklist:

- Unplug televisions, stereos, and clocks.
- Remove all linens from beds.
- Remove all clothes from dressers. (Only hanging clothes can stay in the room.)
- Remove all plants, pets, animals from the house.
- Remove all fresh fruits, fresh vegetables, chocolates, carbonated beverages, wines, and liquors.
- Remove all candles, wax, crayons, lipstick, and other cosmetics that may melt.
- Remove all medicines and vitamins.
- Remove all arts and craft items that are assembled with a hot glue gun.
- Remove all plastic blinds and leave them on the floor.
- Remove all paintings and pictures from the walls.
- Remove all combustible items like oxygen tanks, fire extinguishers and cigarette lighters.

Notes

1. Julia Haines, "These American Cities Have the Worst Bedbug Problems, November 1, 2023, *U.S. News & World Report*, http://tinyurl.com/3rkczfvc.

2. Juan Cabrera, "Learn English Idioms: The Early Bird Gets the Worm," September 29, 2020, Missouri State University blog, http://tinyurl.com/mrmmtmh9.

ACKNOWLEDGMENTS

To my beloved husband, Rico, and cherished children, Chris (Hannah) and Matt (Courtney), your unwavering love and support have been my greatest blessings. This book is a tribute to the light you bring into my life.

A heartfelt thank you to Suzi Fox, whose gentle nudge and belief in my abilities sparked the inspiration to embark on this writing adventure. Your encouragement was the catalyst that set this project in motion.

I extend my deepest appreciation to my dear friends, Lauren, Jan, Kathy, and Jamie, whose uplifting, understanding, and occasional doses of humor kept me grounded and motivated throughout the writing process. Your friendship means the world to me.

A special thank you goes to my editor, Claudia Volkman, whose keen insights, invaluable guidance, and meticulous attention to detail have transformed this manuscript into its best possible form. Your dedication to excellence and unwavering support have made this journey both rewarding and fulfilling.

To all those who have offered their support, encouragement, and expertise along the way, I extend my heartfelt thanks. This book would not have been possible without each of you.

ABOUT THE AUTHOR

 Immerse yourself in the vibrant world of Deanna L. Vigliotta, debut author of the captivating narrative *The Traveling Saleslady Meets Live Bedbugs*. While this marks her inaugural foray into published literature, Deanna's literary prowess has long been evident through her prolific contributions to esteemed senior living publications. Notably, her insightful piece "Holiday Napkins" garnered acclaim as the "top marketplace column" of 2022 by the renowned McKnight's *Senior Living* publication, cementing her status as a thought leader in her field.

Beyond her written endeavors, Deanna is a dynamic public speaker, firm in her belief that storytelling serves as the linchpin to deeper understanding across all subjects. With an illustrious thirty-year career in healthcare sales and management, she brings a wealth of knowledge and insight to her work. Currently serving as the national sales manager for TZMO USA, Inc., a distinguished division of a leading European manufacturer specializing in medical hygiene products, Deanna's passion for helping others shines through in every interaction. Her commitment to serving as a steadfast resource for both colleagues and clientele is unparalleled.

Nestled in the heart of central Florida alongside her beloved husband, Rico, Deanna finds solace and inspiration in the company of her family, which includes her two grown sons and their significant others. She cherishes the moments spent together, embracing the values of love, laughter, and togetherness. Outside of her professional pursuits, Deanna finds joy in the simple pleasures of life— whether it's the tranquility of a leisurely walk, the thrill of exploring new destinations, or the fulfillment found in lifelong learning.

To connect with Deanna and delve more deeply into her world of storytelling and insight, feel free to reach out at deanna@thetravelingsaleslady.com. Join her on a journey where every page brims with warmth, wisdom, and wit.